01

Scott Shaw

Buddha Rose Publications

Copyright © 1985 by Scott Shaw
www.scottshaw.com
All Rights Reserved

No part of this book may be reproduced in any manner without the expressed written permission of the author or the publishing company.

Front Cover Painting by Scott Shaw

First Edition 1985
Second Edition 1989
Third Edition 2011

ISBN 10: 1-877792-20-9
ISBN 13: 978-1-877792-20-5

10 9 8 7 6 5 4 3 2 1

Printed in the United States of America

01

from portable notebooks(s) late
'84, early *'85*

1

in e-o am

I love you in Vietnamese

so she said to me
I wasn't all that interested

2

have I paid the price yet

for your love

or is it
that I must wait
until another time

3

I have to wait a week for you
is it payment for my sins

is it a moment
for all of my lost moments

or is it just time
to live a momentary fantasy

4

I understand
your subtitles

5

to do today:

get L.A. Weekly
gas cap for MG
read computer text
laundry
paint
get black enamel paint
6-volt light bulb for 356

6

I fell like fucking shit today
I am standing here
pumping gas into my 356
at the 76 Union station,
Hermosa Beach
all the clothes I like to wear
are either in the dry cleaners
or dirty
I'm hungry
no money
and now I have to go home
and change clothes
spilled fucking gas on myself

I feel fucked
these words
don't even describe it

and it's hot
and it's winter
and the beach looks nice
and a boat drives by
and it makes me feel more fucked

no boat
and I have to go to Hollywood
to get some money
I have none

my bank is in Hollywood

I feel fucked

7

it seems man always seeks power
over another

first level
    sexual conquest

second level
    assault

third level
    murder

from bad to worse

maybe,
it is only the small minded
who are motivated by this
but it seems one way or another
it rules and guides society

perhaps,
it is brought on by society
or by animal instinct
I don't know
but it is sad

8

slap my face with it
once more

I walk to my P.O. Box
after being hung up on
by a chick
that I don't care about anyway

a call from Spain
don't call me anymore

I go to my P.O. Box
expecting another
rejection notice from a publisher
but it is worse
there is nothing

the ultimate slap in the face

I, I am alone

9

the rays trickle down
like the waves of mercy
in a semi unclean moment
of non-descript pain

10

I sit here in L.A.
a Friday afternoon traffic jam
dying somewhere deep inside
chasing unwanted illusion

illusions
dying
somewhere
deep inside

11

I walk down the street
12:00 o'clock midnight
all alone

I see a girl standing
waiting
she is picked up by
two apparent male friends
on bicycles

they begin to laugh
to joke
to yell

I walk
I hear them behind me

pretty soon
closing the distance gap
1-2-3
THUMP!
they wiped out on *the strand*
the two bicycles
the dudes and the girl
I keep walking

12

it is so hard
to be hung up on
when you've got
no one else to call

all the poets/all the artists
they talk of being alone
but I doubt
if they have experienced it

13

in this foggy night
I cry

14

just a thought of you
in a thoughtless world
trying to grab un-seen wind
that has no boundaries

15

to do today:

Chino
Norton Simon
Arron Bros.
      stretcher bars
      paint
Melrose
take mother to the store

16

do you want me
to be there
for you to run home to

think those thoughts in your mind
I will be there

17

it amazes me
how people
    myself included
talk about things
that they know nothing about
and reach
totally
unfounded
conclusions

all based on speculations,
hearsay, etc.

18

to remain
on the periphery of insanity
neither
stepping to this side or that

19

and the rain
washes our senses
making us senseless
and we pray
for the moment
when the world
will release its hold

20

people love to find excuses
for their psychological problems
and make them sound artistic
make them sound alright

like self-destructive people
who call themselves artists

they say it is all part of the art
etc…

21

car broke down
so I stand here
downtown L.A.
leaning against a wall
checking out the women
who walk by
I stand here
with all the Mexicans
waiting for a bus

22

to do:

slide holders
probably metal boxes
or plastic sheets to hold them

Sears
get a router
chin-up bar

Ole's
new drill

Sportsmart
bike holder

23

tel.
556-2505
557-5446
567-1058-9

telex
k28870wtfed

24

for some reason
I love the inner-city ghetto women
it's not just that they're easy
it's that their whole environment
is easy
it is old/rundown
no one to impress
one can just be themselves
who they are

L.A. isn't like New York
Manhattan it is all the same
and it is chic to be there
L.A. on the other hand
is big
and it is divided

the rich/the white chic
move outwards
leaving the poor
the newly immigrated
to live on the streets
the streets/my home
unwanted as it is
the streets/my home

25

52.45
4.66
28.00
20.00
25.00

26

smoking
is for the fools
and waitresses

27

just studying reality
and other subjective conclusions
or other subjective unions

28

time fades
the picture rapidly

29

I'm into the science of the night

the alone of being

alone
the night
silence

30

San Francisco
well, here I sit...

7:30 AM this morning
I get up
via a phone call
from my main and current
L.A. babe
she rings the line
as always, she says nothing worth
listening too
then to the airport
late, too late
I hurry
but I went to the wrong terminal
couldn't find Air-Cal
I park my truck at United
then/there
I had ten minutes to spare
I walk fast
I get there
no line
very happy/very lucky
then onto the plane
slept most of the way

first-class style
then rent a car
Olds Cutlass
blue/nice
drove to S.F. from SFO
search radio for The-Quake
while driving
little bit lost
than find the India Embassy
I should remember it's location
been there way too many times
to forget where it was
like I did
need new visa
than a little drive
and now at IHOP
today
beautiful rainy day in S.F.
I will walk at the Observatory,
I think
then City Lights
then Chinatown
maybe
romantic day
all alone
just live the sitting here

coffee
and awaiting breakfast

awh, the rain...

31

my attention
gets drawn
as I pour my coffee
over/out of the cup

not too much different than life

32

IHOP
mid-west hick heaven
in California
where all the people
who have mid-west faces
smoke cigarettes
and are waited on
by replanted mid-west waitresses

terrible...

33

walk in the rain
alone in S.F.

no one would understand me
beautiful day
beautiful mind
forget the umbrella
forget everything
but the rain
in S.F.

34

walking
in between the raindrops
hiding
from society

another kind of desire
another wind through my hair

35

overlooking the bay
the ocean
the wind blows gently
the sound
the feeling
only hampered
by the noise of the cars
motion coming and going
how I hate noise

36

soft ocean waves
hard ocean waves
so much different

soft ocean sound
hard ocean sound
so much different

heard in the distance

37

how strong is your shadow ?

does your shadow grow strong ?

38

well, got to the airport
checked in and all
a bit of a hassle
getting to the car rental place
kinda got me angry
but such is life
all done and checked in
maybe 5:30 PM

in the airport
this NY girl
30ish
begins to talk with me
there on business
en route to L.A.
she wants to know my reason
for being there
I tell her
she wants to see
all the stamps in my passport
I show her
she was just begging me
to ask her out
thanx but no thanx

it's funny, desire
when you can have it
and you don't want it
and there is times
when you just want plain lust
with anyone that is there
it is all by the moment
and any other time
I would not have turned her down

the sink at zero-zero
(seek out that story
in my other writings)

but the moment
but all that stinky pussy sex
no thank you
I prefer love
as momentary as it is

my seat on the plane: 9F
I probably have
three and a half feet leg room
so pretty good

awh, life

39

it's funny
there are places
that one may not see locally
for long periods of time
and think nothing of it
but more dramatic/more distant locations
are more prominent in the mind

so the time
it is counted

example:

I have not been to
Huntington Beach
for maybe two years
but I give it no thought
but I count my time
from Japan, Bangkok, Singapore

40

I spoke distant words of memory
heard faint sounds
looked deep into the hidden wind
and cried a Tibet tear

41

and the dreams
keep dreaming

www.ingramcontent.com/pod-product-compliance
Lightning Source LLC
LaVergne TN
LVHW051210080426
835512LV00019B/3193